THE FLY

Also by Miroslav Holub

On the Contrary and other poems (Bloodaxe Books, 1984)
  [translated by Ewald Osers]

MIROSLAV HOLUB

THE FLY

TRANSLATED BY
EWALD OSERS
GEORGE THEINER
IAN & JARMILA MILNER

BLOODAXE BOOKS

ISBN: 1 85224 018 0

First published 1987 by
Bloodaxe Books Ltd,
P.O. Box 1SN,
Newcastle upon Tyne NE99 1SN.

Bloodaxe Books Ltd acknowledges
the financial assistance of Northern Arts.

Typesetting by Bryan Williamson, Manchester.

Printed in Great Britain by
Tyneside Free Press Workshop Ltd, Newcastle upon Tyne.

Acknowledgements

The translations by George Theiner and Ian Milner first appeared in Miroslav Holub's *Selected Poems* (Penguin Modern European Poets, 1967), and are published here by kind permission of Penguin Books Ltd. Those by Ian and Jarmila Milner are taken from *Although* (Jonathan Cape, 1971). The other translations, by Ewald Osers, are published here for the first time.

This selection was made by Miroslav Holub from the following books:

11-17   *Denní služba* / Day duty (1958)
18-25   *Achilles a želva* / Achilles and the tortoise (1960)
26-45   *Slabikář* / Primer (1961)
46-56   *Jdi a otevři dvere* / Go and open the door (1962)
57-71   *Tak zvané srdce* / The so-called heart (1963)
72-75   *Zcela nesoustavná zoologie* / Totally unsystematic zoology (1963)
76-80   *Kam teče krev* / Where the blood flows (1963)
81-96   *Ačkoli* / Although (1969)
97-102   *Beton* / Concrete (1970)

Contents

Cinderella

Cinderella is sorting her peas:
bad ones those, good ones these,
yes and no, no and yes.
No cheating. No untruthfulness.

From somewhere the sound of dancing.
Somebody's horses are prancing.
Somebody's riding in state.

The slipper's no longer too small,
toes have been cut off for the ball.
This is the truth. Never doubt.

Cinderella is sorting her peas:
bad ones those, good ones these,
yes and no, no and yes.
No cheating. No untruthfulness.

Coaches drive to the palace door
and everybody bows before
the self-appointed bride.

No blood is flowing. Just red birds
from distant parts are clearly heard
as, plumage ruffled, they alight.

Cinderella is sorting her peas:
bad ones those, good ones these,
yes and no, no and yes.

No little nuts, no prince that charms
and we all long for mother's arms,
yet there is but one hope:

Cinderella is sorting her peas:
softly as one fits joints together
with fingers gentle as a feather,
or as one kneads the dough for bread.

And though it may be light as air,
merely a song in someone's head
a gossamer of truth is there.

Cinderella is sorting her peas:
bad ones those, good ones these,
yes and no, no and yes,
no cheating in this bout.

She knows that she is on her own.
No helpful pigeons; she's alone.
And yet the peas, they *will* be sorted out.

[EO]

Graves of prisoners

'Jemand erzählt von seiner Mutter…'
R.M. RILKE

Šumava Mountains; bulls' horns locked
in fight on trampled soil
piled into hill and rock.

Deserted frontier, deathbed-like,
an abandoned house nearby.
Resisting maples strike
out for the sky.

A cemetery, crumbling, grey,
black lilac choking the stone.
What have those wolfish rains washed away?
And what have they left alone?

> Below a ruined wall
> four graves still tell a story:
> Kolisan Alexandr,
> Gavril Kondratenko,
> Tatshenko Vladimir,
> Henri Joly.

Prisoners. In nineteen forty-two.
And still on the graves no grass will grow,
as if thin smoke hung over them,
as if their bodies rose up from below.

As if they were holding hands.

Under the rain-drenched maples it seems
as if a fire were flickering gently,
as if someone were sitting there
and listening intently.

Someone with an accordion
on this damp, unhealed clay.
Picks it up. Starts to play.
Someone speaks of some campaign or other.

Someone speaks of his mother.

[EO]

The flypaper

The kitchen's buzzing conscience:
death of the guilty and innocent,

Sisyphuses.

Behold an earthly paradise
without midge, gnat or fly.

Arbeit macht frei.

[EO]

Harbour

But the sea was measured
and chained to the earth.
And the earth was measured
and chained to the sea.

They launched
cranes, lean angels,
they calculated
the wail of widowed sirens,
they foresaw
the nervous unrest of buoys,
they drafted
the labyrinth of routes around the world.

They constructed
the Minotaurs of ships.

They discovered five continents.

The earth was measured
and chained to the sea.
And the sea was measured
and chained to the earth.

All that is left
is a small house above the canal.
A man who spoke softly,
a woman with tears in her eyes.
All that is left is the evening lamp,
the continent of the table,
the tablecloth, a seagull that does not fly away.

All that is left
is a cup of tea,
the deepest ocean in the world.

[GT]

In the microscope

Here too are dreaming landscapes,
lunar, derelict.
Here too are the masses,
tillers of the soil.
And cells, fighters
who lay down their lives
for a song.

Here too are cemeteries,
fame and snow.
And I hear murmuring,
the revolt of immense estates.

[IM]

Pathology

Here in the Lord's bosom rest
the tongues of beggars,
the lungs of generals,
the eyes of informers,
the skins of martyrs,

in the absolute
of the microscope's lenses.

I leaf through Old Testament slices of liver,
in the white monuments of brain I read
the hieroglyphs
of decay.

Behold, Christians,
Heaven, Hell, and Paradise
in bottles.
And no wailing,
not even a sigh.
Only the dust moans.
Dumb is history
strained
through capillaries.

Equality dumb. Fraternity dumb.

And out of the tricolours of mortal suffering
we day after day
pull
threads of wisdom.

[GT]

Night in the streets

They are singing
at the bird-fancier's.
The houses are growing.

A few bricks
are coming away from the cathedral.
Here and there
a feather
or a cat
or dog
falls from the sky.

They are singing
at the bird-fancier's.

The houses are growing.
In their walls runs
the white blood of the just.
On the breath of millions
the moon rises,
the immense heart
rolls night towards day.

It's enough that we are alive.
Are breathing.

Responsible
even for the rotation of the earth.

[IM]

Napoleon

Children, when was
Napoleon Bonaparte born,
asks teacher.

A thousand years ago, the children say.
A hundred years ago, the children say.
Last year, the children say.
No one knows.

Children, what did
Napoleon Bonaparte do,
asks teacher.

Won a war, the children say.
Lost a war, the children say.
No one knows.

Our butcher had a dog
called Napoleon,
says František.
The butcher used to beat him and the dog died
of hunger
a year ago.

And all the children are now sorry
for Napoleon.

[IM/JM]

The corporal who killed Archimedes

With one bold stroke
he killed the circle, tangent
and point of intersection
in infinity.

On penalty
of quartering
he banned numbers
from three up.

Now in Syracuse
he heads a school of philosophers,
squats on his halberd
for another thousand years
and writes:

one two
one two
one two
one two

[IM/JM]

Death in the evening

High, high.

Her last words wandered across the ceiling
like clouds.
The sideboard wept.
The apron shivered
as if covering an abyss.

The end. The young ones had gone to bed.

But towards midnight
the dead woman got up,
put out the candles (a pity to waste them),
quickly mended the last stocking,
found her fifty nickels
in the cinnamon tin
and put them on the table,
found the scissors fallen behind the cupboard,
found a glove
they had lost a year ago,
tried all the door knobs,
tightened the tap,
finished her coffee,
and fell back again.

In the morning they took her away.
She was cremated.
The ashes were coarse
as coal.

[GT]

Five minutes after the air raid

In Pilsen,
twenty-six Station Road,
she climbed to the third floor
up stairs which were all that was left
of the whole house,
she opened her door
full on to the sky,
stood gaping over the edge.

For this was the place
the world ended.

Then
she locked up carefully
lest someone steal
Sirius
or Aldebaran
from her kitchen,
went back downstairs
and settled herself
to wait
for the house to rise again
and for her husband to rise from the ashes
and for her children's hands and feet to be stuck back in place.

In the morning they found her
still as stone,
sparrows pecking her hands.

[GT]

Explosion

Yés;
but then came
bricklayers,
doctors,
carpenters,
     people with shovels,
     people with hopes,
     people with rags,
stroked
the loins of the wild house,
stroked
the pounding heart of space,
stroked the crest of pain

until all the bricks came back,
until all the drops of blood came back,
all the molecules of oxygen

and stone
pardoned stone.

[IM/JM]

Home I.

From amidst last year's cobwebs
she glanced up from a creaking easy-chair:
'You're looking well, boy.'

And wounds were healing,
we were children again,
and no school today.

And when things were at their worst,
with no night and no day
and no up and no down
and we barely dared breathe,

she'd say
from amidst her cobwebs:
'You're looking well boy.'

And wounds would heal before her eyes
even though she was

blind.

[EO]

Voices in the landscape

The mist stays awake.
From infinite distance comes the howling of lemurs.
The grass's soul laughs happily in the moonlight.
And people think the air is crying.

Darkness gnaws at the trees.

The soul of a legless baker
has a story of yeast to tell.
The strung-up forest
sings in the willow slips.
A seamstress climbs
down the thread from
a tubercular room.

Night oxygenated by eternity.

Soldiers,
tunics still white,
playing the hurdygurdy
of level-crossing gates.

The tavern's roar in tiny pebbles.

At the break of day
the ghosts will die
and be finally laid to rest
in a thimble
in loaves of bread,
in cubic metres,
in thresholds
and in door-handles

everlasting
like us.

[EO]

Alphabet

Ten million years
from the Miocene
to the primary school in Ječná Street.

We know everything
from *a* to *z*.

But sometimes the finger stops
in that empty space between *a* and *b*,
empty as the prairie at night,

between *g* and *h*,
deep as the eyes of the sea,

between *m* and *n*,
long as man's birth,

sometimes it stops
in the galactic cold
after the letter *z*,
at the beginning and the end,

trembling a little
like some strange bird.

Not from despair.

Just like that.

[EO]

A history lesson

Kings
like golden gleams
made with a mirror on the wall.

A non-alcoholic pope,
knights without arms,
arms without knights.

The dead like so many strained noodles,
a pound of those fallen in battle,
two ounces of those who were executed,

several heads
like so many potatoes
shaken into a cap –

Geniuses conceived
by the mating of dates
are soaked up by the ceiling into infinity

to the sound of tinny thunder,
the rumble of bellies,
shouts of hurrah,

empires rise and fall
at a wave of the pointer,
the blood is blotted out –

And only one small boy,
who was not paying the least attention,
will ask
between two victorious wars:

And did it hurt in those days too?

[GT]

The sick primer

Even the primer
may
fall sick one day
    because
    the children are good and work hard.
    But that isn't really quite true,
    the leaves drop in the autumn,
    but that isn't really quite true,
    flames burn, the moon shines,
    but that isn't really quite true.
    Dad may work his fingers to the bone,
    but that isn't really quite true,
    this is now and that is later,
    but that isn't really quite true,

even the primer
may
fall sick one day with
what isn't really quite true,
the worst
contagious disease,
with paper fevers,
with black-and-white hallucinations,
with superstitious spots,

wise men
will bandage the primer,
cover the primer,
lock up the primer
    (better a half-truth than nothing),

but the primer
will talk
in its sleep,
    don't believe in ghosts,
    don't believe in plaster,
    in eyes or in ears,
    don't believe in words,

the primer
will talk
in its sleep,
        better a temporary nothing
        than definitive half-truths,
it will call out,
        try a bit harder, for Chrissake,
        get your noddles working,
        don't swallow your own lies,

wise men
will sentence the insane primer
for illiteracy,
        to be set to music,
        to be billed as a poster,
        to be translated
        into a dead language,

and children
themselves
will have to paint a dot,
some will paint the sun,
some will draw a circle
with compasses, for an alpha plus,

and the teacher will say
I shall never get through
testing and marking
that lot.

[EO]

Midday

Day has cast anchor in the shallows.

Trees tremble with happiness,
immortal
butterflies sing.

The sky is sweet
as a face we love
that day.

Children's small voices
tumble down the hillsides.

Sun, song, peace:

something's impending.

[EO]

The rain at night

With mouse-like teeth
the rain gnaws at stone.
The trees parade through the town
like prophets.

Perhaps it's the sobbing
of the monstrous angels of darkness,
perhaps the suppressed laughter
of the flowers out there in the garden,
trying to cure consumption
by rustling.

Perhaps the purring
of the holy drought
under any kind of cover.

An unspeakable time,
when the voice of loudspeakers cracks
and poems
are made not of words
but of drops.

[GT]

The forest

Among the primary rocks
where the bird spirits
crack the granite seeds
and the tree statues
with their black arms
threaten the clouds,

suddenly
there comes a rumble,
as if history
were being uprooted,

the grass bristles,
boulders tremble,
the earth's surface cracks

and there grows

a mushroom,

immense as life itself,
filled with billions of cells
immense as life itself,
eternal,
watery,

appearing in this world for the first

and last time.

[GT]

Haul of fish

The court is in session.

And all that is hidden
shall be revealed.

In the last fish-pond
the last fish
on the dried-up bed
soundlessly dies.

And the terror of the gills
and the terror of slime

contentedly

rise to the skies.

[EO]

Spice

A bay leaf from Baghdad,
pepper from Zanzibar,
marjoram from Casablanca.

These are the smell of home.

The cities' houses exactly
as pictures in the album,
hovels on the desert's edge,
yellowing,
like those tins on the sideboard.

The bewitching taste of distant lands.

[EO]

The fly

She sat on a willow-trunk
watching
part of the battle of Crécy,
the shouts,
the gasps,
the groans,
the tramping and the tumbling.

During the fourteenth charge
of the French cavalry
she mated
with a brown-eyed male fly
from Vadincourt.

She rubbed her legs together
as she sat on a disembowelled horse
meditating
on the immortality of flies.

With relief she alighted
on the blue tongue
of the Duke of Clervaux.

When silence settled
and only the whisper of decay
softly circled the bodies

and only
a few arms and legs
still twitched jerkily under the trees,

she began to lay her eggs
on the single eye
of Johann Uhr,
the Royal Armourer.

And thus it was
that she was eaten by a swift
fleeing
from the fires of Estrées.

[GT]

Shooting galleries

All over the place
shooting galleries arrive,
boys are getting ready
to hunt
tin clowns.

At night
the rifles grind their teeth,
paper roses smell sweet on the graves
of the peeling fallen.

All over the place
shooting galleries leave,
and in trampled grass
a scarlet
drop of blood
remains.

[EO]

Textbook of a dead language

This is a boy.
This is a girl.

The boy has a dog.
The girl has a cat.

What colour is the dog?
What colour is the cat?

The boy and the girl
are playing with a ball.

Where is the ball rolling?

Where is the boy buried?
Where is the girl buried?

Read
and translate
into every silence and every language!

Write
where you yourselves
are buried!

[GT]

The village green

The memorial of our heroes
has crumbled into stone:
the last casualty of the last war.

The sky over that spot
is healing the scar,
the goose fanfare
calls the wounded sward back to life.

But under the ground a mouse
says to another,
about to give birth:
Not here, come a bit farther!

[GT]

Polonius

Behind every arras
he does his duty
unswervingly.
Walls are his ears,
keyholes his eyes.

He slinks up the stairs,
oozes from the ceiling,
floats through the door
ready to give evidence,
prove what is proven,
stab with a needle
or pin on an order.

His poems always rhyme,
his brush is dipped in honey,
his music flutes
from marzipan and cane.

You buy him
by weight, boneless,
a pound of wax flesh,
a pound of mousy philosophy,
a pound of jellied
flunkey.

And when he's sold out
and the left-overs wrapped
in a tasselled obituary,
a paranoid funeral notice,

and when the spore-creating mould
of memory
covers him over,
when he falls
arse-first to the stars,

the whole continent will be lighter,
earth's axis straighten up
and in night's thunderous arena
a bird will chirp in gratitude.

[IM]

Love

Two thousand cigarettes.
A hundred miles
from wall to wall.
An eternity and a half of vigils
blanker than snow.

Tons of words
old as the tracks
of a platypus in the sand.

A hundred books we didn't write.
A hundred pyramids we didn't build.

Sweepings.
Dust.

Bitter
as the beginning of the world.

Believe me when I say
it was beautiful.

[IM]

Bones

We lay aside
　　useless bones,
　　ribs of reptiles,
　　jawbones of cats,
　　the hip-bone of the storm,
　　the wish-bone of Fate.

　　To prop the growing head
　　of Man
We seek
　　a backbone
　　that will stay
　　straight.

[GT]

The geology of man

Some
natural common
cause.

Some
elementary value
of life.

Some goodness
of heart
or liver
or whatever.

These depths are in the sand.

It only takes
a bad storm,
a dash of alcohol,
a drop of grandmother's
superstition

and the flood is here.

Goodness
is orogeny.

Without a magnetic
overburden of necessity
not a hair of sense
is etched.

Only continuous
internal bleeding
coagulating in the fissures
into basalts and granites.

Man
is just drudgery
for two million years.

[EO]

Wings

We have
a microscopic anatomy
of the whale
this
gives
Man
assurance
    WILLIAM CARLOS WILLIAMS

We have
a map of the universe
for microbes,
we have
a map of a microbe
for the universe.

We have
a Grand Master of chess
made of electronic circuits.

But above all
we have
the ability
to sort peas,
to cup water in our hands,
to seek
.the right screw
under the sofa
for hours

This
gives us
wings.

[GT]

A helping hand

We gave a helping hand to grass –
    and it turned into corn.
We gave a helping hand to fire –
    and it turned into a rocket.
Hesitatingly,
cautiously,
we give a helping hand
to people,
to some people...

[GT]

Ode to joy

You only love
when you love in vain.

Try another radio probe
when ten have failed,
take two hundred rabbits
when a hundred have died:
only this is science.

You ask the secret.
It has just one name:
again.

In the end
a dog carries in his jaws
his image in the water,
people rivet the new moon,
I love you.

Like caryatids
our lifted arms
hold up time's granite load

and defeated
we shall always win.

[IM]

The door

Go and open the door.
　Maybe outside there's
　a tree, or a wood,
　a garden,
　or a magic city.

Go and open the door.
　Maybe a dog's rummaging.
　Maybe you'll see a face,
or an eye,
or the picture
　　　　　of a picture.

Go and open the door.
　If there's a fog
　it will clear.

Go and open the door.
　Even if there's only
　the darkness ticking,
　even if there's only
　the hollow wind,
　even if
　　　　nothing
　　　　　　is there,
go and open the door.

At least
there'll be
a draught.

[IM]

Evening idyll with a protoplasm

Over the houses spreads
the eczema of twilight,
the evening news bulletin
creeps across the façades,
the beefburger is singing.

A protoplasm called
well-that's-life
bulges from all the windows,
tentacles with sharp-eyed old hags' heads,
it engulfs a pedestrian,
penetrates into beds across the road,
swallowing tears and fragments of quarrels,
pregnancies and miscarriages,
splashing used cars and television sets,
playing havoc with the price of eggs,
slimily puffing itself with adulteries,
crossing off plotting spores of
things-were-different-in-our-day.

And even after dark it phosphoresces
like a dead sea drying up

between featherbed, plum jam and stratosphere.

[EO]

A few very clever people

Their words were pins,
their silences needles.

Night with cold hands
was leaning on
the unstitched animal of the world.

And walking home
they kicked
            a loaf
from one corner
                to the next.

[EO]

The teacher

The earth rotates,
                    says the young pupil.
Not so, the earth rotates,
                    says the teacher.

The hills are turning green,
                    says the young pupil.
Not so, the hills are turning green,
                    says the teacher.

Twice two is four,
                    says the young pupil.
Not so, twice two is four,
                    the teacher corrects him.

Because the teacher knows best.

[EO]

The best room, or interpretation of a poem

And now tell it to me
in other words,
says the stuffed owl
to the fly
which, with a buzz,
is trying with its head
to break through the window-pane.

[EO]

Žito the magician

To amuse His Royal Majesty he will change water into wine.
Frogs into footmen. Beetles into bailiffs. And make a Minister
out of a rat. He bows, and daisies grow from his finger-tips.
And a talking bird sits on his shoulder.

There.

Think up something else, demands His Royal Majesty.
Think up a black star. So he thinks up a black star.
Think up dry water. So he thinks up dry water.
Think up a river bound with straw-bands. So he does.

There.

Then along comes a student and asks: Think up sine alpha
greater than one.

And Žito grows pale and sad: Terribly sorry. Sine is
between plus one and minus one. Nothing you can do about that.
And he leaves the great royal empire, quietly weaves his way
through the throng of courtiers, to his home
                                    in a nutshell.

[GT]

Inventions

Wise men in long white togas come forward during the
festivities, rendering account of their labours,
and King Belos listens.

O, mighty King, says the first, I've made a pair of wings
for your throne. You shall rule from the air. –
Then applause and cheering follow, the man is
richly rewarded.

O, mighty King, says the second, I've made a self-acting
dragon which will automatically defeat your foes. –
Then applause and cheering follow, the man is
richly rewarded.

O, mighty King, says the third, I've made a destroyer
of bad dreams. Now nothing shall disturb your royal sleep. –
Then applause and cheering follow, the man is
richly rewarded.

But the fourth man only says: Constant failure has dogged
my steps this year. Nothing went right. I bungled everything
I touched. – Horrified silence follows and
the wise King Belos is silent too.

It was ascertained later that the fourth man was
Archimedes.

[GT]

Merry-go-round

Some ride on chestnut mares
to plum-jam Argentina,
some ride in atomic trams
into space
without holding on.

The music oozes from the lowering sky
like the past century
wailing overhead
for all we used to love
and will love yet.

And the riders on horseback
and the red tram's passengers
will be
       aviators
            and engineers.

But the little boy who
crouches to watch the electric motor below,
the electric motor driving the noontide witch,
the gingerbread cottages
and the sclerotic
cardboard princess,

the little boy
who remarked –
why, this things runs as smooth as shit –
that little boy
will be a poet.

[EO]

Poem technology

It is
    a fuse,
you light
somewhere in the grass,
or in a cave,
or in a third-rate
        saloon.

The little flame races
among the blades,
among the startled butterflies,
among terrified stones, among sleepy tankards,
racing,

growing a little or vanishing
like pain in a supernumerary finger,
hissing, spluttering,
halting
      in microscopic vertigo,

but right at the end
        it explodes,
a boom as from a cannon,
tatters of words fly through the universe,
the day's walls reverberate,

but even if
no rock is burst
someone will say at least –
      Hell, something's happened!

[EO]

The bell

In this house no one has a bell. Everyone
recognises his visitors through the wall,
if any come at all.

Only the oldest woman, a lady lonely as a rat, had
a shrilly-tuned bell
fixed to her doorpost,
so it could stay silent year
after year.
Yet one day on the stairs there'll be a white
unicorn and he will ring without expecting an answer.

And the old lady will open her door and call
after him:
Thank you, unicorn!

[EO]

Casualty

They bring us crushed fingers,
mend it, doctor.
They bring burnt-out eyes,
hounded owls of hearts,
they bring a hundred white bodies,
a hundred red bodies,
a hundred black bodies,
mend it, doctor,
on the dishes of ambulances they bring
the madness of blood
the scream of flesh,
the silence of charring,
mend it, doctor.

And while we are suturing
inch after inch,
night after night,
nerve to nerve,
muscle to muscle,
eyes to sight,
they bring in
even longer daggers,
even more thunderous bombs,
even more glorious victories,

idiots.

[EO]

Riders

Over the kind earth twisted like Christmas-bread
over the white earth inscribed grammatically

in nonpareil, brevier, pica,
over the wise earth resounding
like the skull of St Augustine,
over the earth smooth as satin
shrouding the bosom of mystery,

four riders are galloping
on plump white horses,
four rosy-cheeked riders with forget-me-not eyes,
with velvet hands,
with lyres, sugar-basins,
and classics,

one of them lectures,
another one makes love,
the third sings praises,
the fourth gazes into the distance.

The earth undulates slightly behind them,
like the skin of a water snake,
and in the marks of their hooves
grey smallpox erupts.

These will be
the four riders
of the Apocalypse.

[GT]

Discobolus

But
before his final throw
someone whispered to him
from behind
    – Just a moment,
    we still have to discuss this
    purely as a matter of form,
    – You don't know the situation,
    comrade,

    In principle we welcome
    your initiative,
    but you must understand

    – We have to insist on
    fundamental
    agreement
    for every throw,

he felt
the soft Sudanese reed
wind round his wrist,
he wanted to cry out
but
his mouth
was suddenly filled
with the candy-floss of the evening sky,
his muscles swelled
like Thessalian granite,
yet
there was really no point in it,
    – Forward there,
    someone said,
    make way, please,
    Demosthenes
    will throw now,
and Demosthenes
took a grain of sand from under his tongue
and neatly
flicked it in the other's eye,

– Hurrah, one more
world record,
they shouted,

desperate maddened nameless
Discobolus
again swung down
low from the knees,
but he was
already stone
and saw
only a single
huge grain of sand
from horizon to horizon.

So he stood there.

And round the corner
came
the first school excursions
led
by the finest pedagogues,
who referred especially
to the play of the shoulders,
the courageous human heart
and the proud pace forward
on the way
to eternity.

[IM]

The new house

No fiery writing on the wall.
No hair
growing out of the ceiling.
No door-knobs
turned by the dead from outside.

No black thoughts in the chimney.
No shadowy chickens in the attic
or under the cupboards.

Far from it.

Latex, vinyl tiles,
elastic dreams,
the kind of house
each of us might
lay a metaphorical brick for.

Only make sure the floors creak,
comrades,
only make sure the floors creak
                as when the world
                develops wrinkles,

only make sure the floors creak
when we wander
from room to room,
worried.

[EO]

On the building site of a hostel
a report

Among pools of earth,
in a chain reaction of bricks,
between the decaying milk-teeth of concrete blocks

has just been hatched
a grey, two-phase
coffin.

(Wipe your feet)

Enter
a dignified museum
of the gall stones
of emptiness.

(Quiet please)

Fingers of piping explore the hollows
and the Monday morning howl
is everywhere.

(No spitting)

Above the bunk
a single bulb rages
suspended
from a concrete sky.

And on a nail
driven into flesh
shipwrecked socks and brassières
are drying.

(No sliding in the corridors)

We met
staring girls' eyes,
wandering like bugs over the plaster
and we asked,
what is love
and
shall we soon be young?

[GT]

Man cursing the sea

Someone
just climbed to the top of the cliff
and started cursing the sea:

Stupid water, stupid pregnant water,
slimy copy of the sky,
hesitant hoverer between the sun and the moon,
pettifogging reckoner of shells,
fluid, loud-mouthed bull,
fertilising the rocks with his blood,
suicidal sword
splintering itself on any promontory,
hydra, fragmenting the night,
breathing salty clouds of silence,
spreading jelly-like wings
in vain, in vain,
gorgon, devouring its own body,

water, you absurd flat skull of water –

Thus for a while he cursed the sea,
which licked his footprints in the sand
like a wounded dog.

And then he came down
and stroked
the small immense stormy mirror of the sea.

There you are, water, he said,
and went his way.

[GT]

The cat

Outside it was night
like a book without letters.
And the eternal dark
dripped to the stars through the sieve of the city.

I said to her
do not go
you'll only be trapped
and bewitched
and will suffer in vain.

I said to her
do not go
why want
nothing?

But a window was opened
and she went,

a black cat into the black night,
she dissolved,
a black cat in the black night,
she just dissolved

and no one ever saw her again.
Not even she herself.

But you can hear her
sometimes,
when it's quiet
and there's a northerly wind
and you listen intently
to your own self.

[GT]

Fog

The last road has fallen.
From every corner of the breathing fields
the triumphant sea draws nearer
and rocks in its waves
the voices of goldfinches
and the voices of the town.

We are a long way
from space and time,
we come upon the bobbing silhouettes
of stray dinosaurs
and the rayed shadows of Martians
who cannot see for fear.

You have something more to say, but
I do not understand you:
between us stretches
the enormous body of reality
and from its severed head
bubble the clots
of white blood.

[IM]

Night at the observatory

It was thawing.
As if the Avars
were attacking underground.

They stood leaning in the shadows,
his finger discovered
an inch
of unknown gentle country
beneath her left shoulder,

Atlantis, he said,
Atlantis.

Above the fields the wires hissed like iguanas.
A car's horn faded on the air
like a voice from Greek tragedy.
Behind the walls the guard paced back and forth.
Hares were sniffing the distant town.
Wood rotted in the ground.
The Avars were winning.
Trees cracked at the joints.
The wind came and veered off.
They kissed.

From somewhere a rock was falling
its second thousand years.
And the stars were taking in
signals on a frequency of ten megacycles,
beamed to a civilisation
which had died
just before the dawn
of eternity.

[IM]

Prince Hamlet's milk tooth

His tooth fell out milky as
   a dandelion
and everything began to fall,
   as if a rosary had broken,
   as if the string of time had snapped,
and it was downhill going all the way;
round the corner the hearse-driver's coming from his dinner
blind horse in the lead, he jolts along.
Hamlet, we're on our way.

No time now except quickly
   learn to add and multiply,
   learn to cheat and whisper answers,
   to smoke and make love,
   lay in stocks of permanganate
   and naphthalene,
there won't be any more.
And we're on our way, Hamlet.

At dusk you hear the drunken revels of the Danes
   and the trampling of the pollinated flowers,
at dawn the typewriters tap out
   piles of loyalty checks
   with skeleton fingers,
at noon the paper tigers roar
   and commissions are counting up races,
   what will be left for seed
   when it falls.
Hamlet, we're on our way.

But we'll put a bird on our heads
   instead of a soldier's cap, won't we?
We shall walk through the park
   and in the shadow of a red rock
(come in under the shadow of this red rock)
   we shall learn
   to think it over
   just in a small way,
   the way the moss grows,

the way the wash-tubs soak up water,
or we'll take a walk
  five minutes beyond the town,
  growing smaller and smaller,
  a pace-maker on our hearts
  set to an easy rhythm
so we can eat our cake and have it too,
we'll take the oath a little
  and lie a little,
  just from want of not lying,

we heroic lads, salt of the earth,
with our muddled hopes
that one fine day
  we'll damn well prove our salt,
Hamlet.

And keep that tooth of yours.
There won't be any more.

[IM]

Love in August

By an Aztec path
        your hand roamed
        over my chest.
The sun burst out like the egg
        of a pterodactyl
and the aspens rustled
        in a wooden proto-language.
All this has happened before.

The jellied landscape
        was lined with happiness
You worshipped me
        as the goddess of warm rain.

But in every corner of our eyes
        stood one of Maxwell's demons,
allowing the molecules of
        growth and decay
to pass there and back.

And all around us, all around,
        all around,
behind excoriated corneas
        unceasingly,
        like a level behind glass,
        entropy rose
        in a meaningless random universe.

All this has happened before.

All this is yet to happen.

[EO]

And what's new

And what is new in the snow?
Footmarks diverging.
Golden patches, nacre patches,
as on the fleece of butchered lambs.

And what is new in the sand?
Distant cities,
a pillar rising from each.
Some kind of Lot's wife,
turning back,
gently petrifying.

And what is new in the mirror?
Breasts like a pair of calves,
twins of the doe.
And King Solomon
telling lies.

And what is new within?
Like the fine hair-thread of a galvanometer,
like a river's minute source,
someone is thinly laughing.
And therefore exists.

[EO]

What the heart is like

Officially the heart
is oblong, muscular,
and filled with longing.

But anyone who has painted the heart knows
that it is also

spiked like a star
and sometimes bedraggled
like a stray dog at night
and sometimes powerful
like an archangel's drum.

And sometimes cube-shaped
like a draughtsman's dream
and sometimes gaily round
like a ball in a net.

And sometimes like a thin line
and sometimes like an explosion.

And in it is
only a river,
a weir
and at most one little fish
by no means golden.

More like a grey
jealous
loach.

It certainly isn't noticeable
at first sight.

Anyone who has painted the heart knows
that first he had to
discard his spectacles,
his mirror,

throw away his fine-point pencil
and carbon paper

and for a long while
walk
outside.

[EO]

The end of the world

The bird had come to the very end of its song
and the tree was dissolving under its claws.

And in the sky the clouds were twisting
and darkness flowed through all the cracks
into the sinking vessel of the landscape.

Only in the telegraph wires
a message still
crackled:

C–·—o———m——e· h···o———m——e·
y—·——o———u··— h···a·—v···—e·
a·— s···o———n–.

[EO]

Death of a sparrow

A sparrow's death
is quite tiny,
grey,
with minute
wiry claws.

And dust
and the end of hopping
is calling now.
And the empty air
is closing its eyes and
calling now.
Mother is picking over
the thinnest good-night squeak and
calling,
a shadow is flying up and
calling,
surely we're not staying here,
roars the setting sun,
quick, soon there'll be decay,
all the world's tenderness
insistently requests,
let's go!

And at that moment
it just isn't
possible.

[EO]

Jesters

Where do fools go?

Where do fools sleep?

What do fools eat?

What do fools do
when no one
but no one at all
laughs any more

Mummy?

[EO]

A boy's head

In it there is a space-ship
and a project
for doing away with piano lessons.

And there is
Noah's ark,
which shall be first.

And there is
an entirely new bird,
an entirely new hare,
an entirely new bumble-bee.

There is a river
that flows upwards.

There is a multiplication table.

There is anti-matter.

And it just cannot be trimmed.

I believe
that only what cannot be trimmed
is a head.

There is much promise
in the circumstance
that so many people have heads.

[IM]

Injection

You asked
>   what was the meaning of the drop and
>   what did the rabbits feel
>   when every second
>   bore witness against them.

Just look,
>   with three-inch boots
>   judgement arrives
>   and like a voice crying out from the depths
>   blood now appears.
>   (How else could the heart
>   swear an oath?)

And in that glassy silence,
>   concurring by a mere movement,
>   we feel in our finger-tips
>   the weight of life
>   and a strange joy in
>   being free
>   to ask

Without answers.

[EO]

Suffering

Ugly creatures, ugly grunting creatures,
Completely concealed under the point of the needle,
   behind the curve of the Research Task Graph,
Disgusting creatures with foam at the mouth,
   with bristles on their bottoms,
One after the other
They close their pink mouths
They open their pink mouths
They grow pale
Flutter their legs
   as if they were running a very
   long distance,

They close ugly blue eyes,
They open ugly blue eyes
   and
   they're
   dead.

But I ask no questions,
no one asks any questions.

And after their death we let the ugly creatures
   run in pieces along the white expanse
   of the paper electrophore
We let them graze in the greenish-blue pool
   of the chromatogram
And in pieces we drive them for a dip
   in alcohol
   and xylol
And the immense eye of the ugly animal god
   watches their every move
   through the tube of the microscope
And the bits of animals are satisfied
like flowers in a flower-pot
   like kittens at the bottom of a pond
   like cells before conception.
But I ask no questions,
   no one asks any questions,

Naturally no one asks
Whether these creatures wouldn't have preferred
     to live all in one piece,
     their disgusting life
     in bogs
     and canals,
Whether they wouldn't have preferred to eat
     one another alive,
Whether they wouldn't have preferred to make love
     in between horror and hunger,
Whether they wouldn't have preferred to use
     all their eyes and pores to perceive
     their muddy stinking little world
Incredibly terrified,
Incredibly happy
In the way of matter which can do no more.

But I ask no questions,
     no one asks any questions,
Because it's all quite useless,
Experiments succeed and experiments fail,
Like everything else in this world,
     in which the truth advances
     like some splendid silver bulldozer
     in the tumbling darkness,

Like everything else in this world,
     in which I met a lonely girl
     inside a shop selling bridal veils,
In which I met a general covered
     with oak leaves,
In which I met ambulance men who could find no
     wounded,
In which I met a man who had lost
     his name,
In which I met a glorious and famous, bronze,
     incredibly terrified rat,
In which I met people who wanted to lay down
     their lives and people who wanted to lay down
     their heads in sorrow,
In which, come to think of it, I keep meeting my
     own self at every step.

Truth

He left, infallible, the door itself
                was bruised as he
                hit the mark.
We two sat awhile
                the figures in the documents
                staring at us like
                green huge-headed beetles
                out of the crevices of evening.
The books stretched
                their spines,
the balance weighed just for the fun of it
                and the glass beads in the necklace
                of the god of sleep whispered together
                in the scales.

'Have you ever been right?' one of us asked.
'I haven't.'

Then we counted on.
It was late
And outside the smokey town, frosty and purple, climbed to the stars.

[GT]

Reality

The small worms of pain still wriggled
   in the limpid air,
The trembling died away and
Something in us bowed low before
    the fact of the operating-table
    the fact of the window
    the fact of space
    the fact of steel
    with seven blades.

The silence was inviolable
   like the surface of a mirror.

Though we wanted to ask
Where the blood was flowing
And
Whether you were still dead,
   darling.

[IM]

Two

Once again
it's the headlong fall
from a crashing astrojet
through the frozen void,
clouds rip the clothes from limbs
and the deafening earth approaches
like a furious new formation,
like the ball from a schizophrenic cannon.

And suddenly – having landed –
and suddenly – broken in two –
and suddenly sunk
one in the other
we are
imprints of earth in earth
and black naphtha gushes from us
river-bed of a chance apartment
and trickles into the eyes
of the avenging angels
pinched in the door-posts.

And then nothing for us
except night
and then nothing for us
except dawn
and the desolate glory of aeronauts
who have lost their wings
in an unknown foreign country.

[IM/JM]

The gift of speech

He spoke:
his round mouth opened
and shut in the manner
of a fish's song.
A bubbling hiss
could be heard
as the void
rushed in headlong
like marsh gas.

[EO]

Oxidation

An invisible flame hovers over the tables.
Eager compounding of elements
of something with nothing,
of something that isn't said
with something that is,
a hidden endothermic filth.

The process continues
in one ear
out of the other,
the brain grinds the poisoned corn
and behind the glass wall a big sewer-rat
swells like
a pink-faced barbers' patron;
gentle, continuous opening of the veins.

We grow, turning to ashes.

And into the wrinkles, monotype
of a body foreign to one's own,
settle the oxides of silence
and the hydroxides of resignation.

Doesn't matter.

There won't be any gold. The philosopher's stone
is not in the plan.
Smoke from the copybooks and drawings falls into the mouth.
Not having words, we applaud.

And inside,
inside this retort of human skin
a huge ashen statue forms,
with tear-rimmed eyes
and white trembling lips
which at night when
roots dance and a star whistles
repeat the empty ashen primeval word
Later Later Later Later.

[IM/JM]

The root of the matter

I

Faust
or anyone
clumsy enough to be
wise,
anyone who bends the nail
at the first stroke,
anyone who forgets to buy
his ticket or
show his pass
right at the start of the journey,
anyone who can be done out of an ounce
of his half-pound of butter,
in short Faust
takes a walk
(before Easter)
beyond the town, stepping into puddles
he would have rather
avoided,
strolls against the stream of passers-by, tags on to
a crowd which
is cheering, more or less, because
the weather's either cloudy or set fair
and after all
There is nothing to do
except cheer
strolls and shares their mood,
finally
Some mistakes are now mistakes
others are still virtues
walks around like a grandfather clock
out of its case and forgetting to chime,
Nothing has happened but me
always saw it coming
walks around like a run-down battery
on a movable pavement,
listens to the voices from above,

Birds of prey do not sing
   listens to the voices from below,
Are you looking for the meaning of life?
And how are you off for garlic?
   he takes the grey road past the cement works,
   he takes the red road past the slaughter-house,
   he takes the blue road past the lake,
   he takes the banned road past the council offices,
   he takes the green road past the playground
        yelling mindless bodies rolling on the ground –
Youth is no argument.
Age even less
   walks and thinks but rather just
        walks
Thinking is natural
only when there is nothing else
to do

II

   And at last
        (naturally)
   he meets a black poodle
        running around in smaller and
        smaller circles
like an ominous spider
        spinning its vast web.

   – Look, now we shall see
   the poodle's true kernel,
   the root of the matter,
   says Faust and hurries off
        home.
   And the poodle circles
   like a carrier raven,
For keeping one's balance
wings are best
   like a cat, like a mouse,
   like a black-burning bush,
There is poetry in everything. That
is the biggest argument
against poetry

like the ardent hump of the horizon
The hump and other survivals
of the past
   and at the same moment the kindly stoniness of the milestone,
Infallibility and other maladies
of adolescence
   like the Marathon runner
   and yet like himself
(But the root of the matter is not
in the matter itself)
   like the demon that denies,
The more negative the type
the more often it says yes
   like a fallen angel,
Fall and you shall not
be shaken
   like the forefinger of the nether darkness.
But the root of the matter is not
in the matter itself
   Faust hurries home,
   the circles are growing smaller like the noose
         tightening round the neck of a mystery.
   And when Faust sees his house before him
   he gropes for his always missing
         bunch of keys,
   ready to make the sign of the cross,
Is the cross more human
than a straight line?
   or the sign of the straight line,
From criticism of the straight line we get
the dash
   or the sign of the heart,
How many organs are called
heart?
   the sign of the heart on the palm,
Heart, yes, but where do we have
the palm?
   As he's entering his house
   and the poodle's crossing the street eager
   as a stone about to become
         a star,

suddenly
like a knife that falls
        half-blade into the ground
a bus slips through
and
the poodle's run over and dies.

Faust has the cold shivers,
pushed out of history
by a grain of sand,
by a hundredweight of stupidity.

III

The root of the matter is not
in the matter itself
    Grandma used to say
    a man who makes no mistakes makes nothing
    but some sort of termite always
            lurks in the kneading-trough
            of every holy eve

Faust lifts the poodle up
and the blood, like a chasuble put on
        over the head,
runs down at his feet

Keys chanced upon he goes and
opens the house and corridor
and study and the evening
confronting the cosmos.

And he sets down the poodle on his opened book
and the letters drink up the blood with gullets unassuaged
        for centuries,
and the pages suck it in through the skin of their unconsciousness
and it is like
a clown's red cap
on the flat skull of literature,
like a set of illuminated
        initials
after the letter Z.

Howl! You won't have any
trouble with your spelling

IV

Faust, without making light, since pain
      itself gives out the reflected light
      of death,
stands there, nonplussed, and says:
      Dog and nothing but a dog,
      who might have been the allegory of creation
      and are no more than the very meaning of death,
who might have been the annunciator
of another and are no more than
crunched bones,

      dog and nothing but a dog, black, white or other,
      empty-handed messenger, because there is no
      mystery
      except the thread which from our hands
      leads round the far side of things, round the collar of the landscape
      and up the sleeve of a star.
The root of the matter is not
in the matter itself
      dog and nothing but a dog,
      with your eyes gazing into
      the sweet shell of terror,
      stay, you are so fair.
Verweile doch, du bist
so schön
      And Faust feels he loves the dog with a love
      whose essence is hopelessness just as
      hopelessness has its essence in love,
      knows what he should do but cannot,
      not having a bandage
      nor
      a veterinary's licence
      nor
      the right to redress the acts of omnibuses

The root of the matter is not
in the matter itself and often
not
in our hands
    Faust merely knows.
    In the distance a siren wails
        and bells die on the air,
    it is long after Easter,
    Wagner comes in
        to ask after his health,
The good man will live
so that on Judgement Day
he can discourse on the virtues
of naphthalene
    the dog is stretched out and his pupils
        span the horizon
    and the pages of the book beneath him quiver
        like white whispering lips.

    And Faust knows
    that he will not speak of it,
    and if so only by a comma,
    only by a word in a big new book.
    It is really something like
        a coat of grey fur over the soul,
        like the uniform the unknown soldier
        wears inside him.

    And so he goes and starts a painting,
    or a gay little song,
    or a big new book.
Nothing has happened but we
always saw it coming
    All in all India ink
        is the blood's first sister
    and song is just as final
        as life and death
    and equally without allegory,
        without transcendence
        and without fuss.

[IM]

Wisdom

But poetry should never be a thicket,
no matter how delightful, where
the frightened fawn of sense could hide.
      And this is a story of wisdom,
              allied with the roots of life
      And therefore
          in the dark
          and blind.
      A small boy not yet bound
            by the hempen fetters of speech,
      With only ten jingling words
          on his tongue.
      But already in the iron shirt of sickness,
            heavier than a man could bear upright,
      In a white box resembling a glass mountain,
          from which all knights
          tumble head over heel –
There's nothing in the mind that
hasn't been in life.

      (At that time
          tubercular meningitis
          still occurred.)
      On Christmas Eve he got his first
          toys, a giraffe and a red car.
      And in the corridor – far from this
          continent – stood a small Christmas tree
          with tears in its eyes.
There's nothing in life that
hasn't been in the mind.

      And the little boy played, amidst
          symptoms and in the blue valley
          of the fever chart,
      And between two lumbar punctures,
          not unlike to
          being crucified,

He played with his giraffe and his red car,
 which represented
 his crown jewels of time,
 all Christmases and
 all the Punches of the world.
And when we asked him
 what else he would like
He said with a feverish gaze
 from the beyond:
Nothing else.
Wisdom is not in multitude
but in one

 (At that time
 meningitis was still
 fatal.)
It was a very white Christmas,
 snow down to the roots,
 frost up to the sky,
And the glass mountain's tremor
 perceptible under our hands.

And he just played.

[EO]

Encyclopaedia: sum of all knowledge

A giant brown-and-white bull
suspended on chains
by his dislocated hind-leg,
its prolapsed belly
contracted in spasm,

is dragged with its twitching mouth along the ground
and slowly butchered
over a leaky sump.

The giant eye, protruded,
is turning inward,

where some fingernail
ceaselessly gropes,
to discover
what is

β-glucuronidase.

[EO]

Annunciation

It could have been a stray neighing of the night
        outside beneath the window
        as the fire burnt low.
It could have been Jericho's trumpets,
it could have been a chorus
        of hunchbacks under the snow,
it could have been an oak's word to the willows,
and it could have been the pecking of a mocking-bird
        under an owl's wing.
It could have been the judgement of an archangel
and it could have been a newt's evil prophecy.
It could have been the weeping of our only love.

But the functionary at the table turned to us
        and said:
Listen: It is necessary for you to listen.
Listen more resolutely.
let us listen, listen, he listens,
they listen, more resolutely,
more resolutely listen,
lis ten lis ten,
LISTEN,
L i s t e n to us –

And so we didn't hear a damn thing.

[IM/JM]

We who laughed

We were expelled
from the classroom, the square,
gaming-house,
stock exchange, market-place,
television screen and
gilt frame,
and from any
history,
    we
       who laughed.

The city swelled in importance
by two floors
and the phone-tapping devices
tapped better
(in the silence)
and the gatekeeper
kept better guard
and love reached for a knife
and the knife reached for blood
(in the silence)
and the rats became still more
like rats (who never laugh)
while we were expelled,
    we
       who laughed.
Some pterodactyls
circled the heavy sky
and horsetail and club-moss
grew in the flower-pots
and an elegiac mastodon
watched from the town hall
to see if we were returning
    we
       who laughed.

We were not returning.
We walked the worn paving-stones
of the unending street

between the warehouse and the factories,
between the machine-tool shop and the scrap heaps,
between the graffiti walls
and the empty houses,
steps, steps, steps,
through the spindled space·
between bushes, between molehills
and
minefields
and
someone stumbled
in the silence . . . and then nothing. Only silence.
That's why we laughed.

[IM/JM]

Anatomy of a leap into the void

A.   Use of the lift
going up
is permitted, provided

B.   Use of the lift
going down
is not permitted, provided

C.   Use of the lift
going up is

D.   Use of the lift
going down is not

E.   Use of the lift
going up

F.   Use of the lift
going

G.   Use of the lift

H.   Is   Is not

I.   Use

J.   U——

[EO]

Subway station

This evening   Mr Howard T. Lewis,
of unknown address,   gloomy and tired,
wearing a grey overcoat and brown hat,
having decided to take   the BMT, Canarsie Line,
met   at the last station on 8th Ave.
a man   in a grey overcoat and brown hat
whose face,   gloomy and tired, was
the face of Mr   Howard T. Lewis,
while by the barrier   at the end of the empty platform
stood a man   in a grey overcoat, of gloomy appearance,
whose face   was also the face
of Howard T. Lewis   and   gazed dumbly
at the bottom of the dirty steps   down which came
a man in a brown hat,   gloomy and tired,
with a face that was the face of Howard T. Lewis.

And then   through the worn wooden spokes
of the turnstile   came a woman, tired and gloomy,
of unknown address   with a handbag and in a brown
hat   whose face was the face
of all men   and therefore also of Howard T. Lewis and
the steps in the distance   and the nervously muffled steps
near by, steps   of figures bowed by the murkiness
and pale from the light were the steps
of Howard T. Lewis, steps   from an unknown address
to   an unknown address,   now and then
the turnstile turned again   with a snap like a head
dropping in the basket,   or behind the barrier
could be seen   a figure without sex and of no
address,   but otherwise completely like
Howard T. Lewis,   steps   were heard,
heads,   spokes,   distances,   lights   and tunnels
sucked in the sign   8th Ave.   8th Ave.   8th Ave.
in droning crescendo.

When the train left   a stray wind
scattered the pages of a paper   in which there was a report on
        the unknown
address,   fate   and identification
of a man   in a grey overcoat and brown hat,
gloomy and tired.

[IM/JM]

Bull fight

Someone runs about,
someone scents the wind,
someone stomps the ground, but it's hard.

Red flags flutter
and on his old upholstered jade the picador
with infirm lance
scores the first wound.

Red blood spurts between the shoulder-blades.

Chest about to split,
tongue stuck out to the roots.
Hooves stomp of their own accord.

Three pairs of the bandoleros in the back.
And a matador is drawing his sword
over the railing.

And then someone (blood-spattered, all in)
stops and shouts:
Let's go, quit it,
let's go, quit it,
let's go over across the river and into the trees,
let's go across the river and into the trees,
let's leave the red rags behind,
let's go some other place,

thus he shouts,
or wheezes,
or whispers,

and the barriers roar and
no one understands because
everyone feels the same about it,

the black-and-red bull is going to fall
and be dragged away,
and be dragged away,
and be dragged away,

without grasping the way of the world,
without having grasped the way of the world,
before he has grasped the way of the world.

[IM/JM]

Planet

The module made more like a crash-landing.
And on the planet – only fused rocks
and tinder, no spark of life.

Booming.

But the first guards were murdered.
The bodies gored by fangs
were buried in vain. In the black daylight
they vanished immediately from the stone graves
and next day attacked the living.

They felt that some sort of principle,
vampire in spirit, was waiting here to use
the bodies, brains and thoughts
for ends which, like darkness, like spin, like laughter,
were fathomless.

And others were devoured and others
among the gored dead stalked the living.
Until it was no longer clear who
still had the original life in him.

The planet stood like the howling of wolves
petrified in timelessness.

There was no point in pretending to be crabs.
They knew, and it knew through them.
They repaired the module and set out for Earth.
Perhaps still human, perhaps also vampires.

And it's not known whether they ever landed.
And it's not known what did land here.
Maybe there are only
symptoms. And booming.
And the strange activity of dead idiots.

[IM/JM]

The clowns

They jumped. They stamped the ground.
Shrank. Crawled through the retina.
Swelled. Got stuck
          in an indicative clause.

They growled. They sang.
Founded a flea circus
and crawled into it.

They blossomed. They wilted.
Flew in a pumpkin and down a hair.
So that
          they reached the roots.

They rang the bell. They put the lights out.
Dodged the curtain calls.
Gobbled up cap and bells.
Consequently
          they were appointed

supervisors of the Clowns.

[IM/JM]

WRITERS PUBLISHED BY

BLOODAXE BOOKS

FLEUR ADCOCK
BASIL BUNTING
ANGELA CARTER
JOHN CASSIDY
EILÉAN NÍ CHUILLEANÁIN
STEWART CONN
DAVID CONSTANTINE
JENI COUZYN
HART CRANE
ADAM CZERNIAWSKI
PETER DIDSBURY
JOHN DREW
HELEN DUNMORE
DOUGLAS DUNN
STEPHEN DUNSTAN
G.F. DUTTON
LAURIS EDMOND
STEVE ELLIS
RUTH FAINLIGHT
EVA FIGES
TONY FLYNN
PAMELA GILLILAN
ANDREW GREIG
TONY HARRISON
MIROSLAV HOLUB
FRANCES HOROVITZ
DOUGLAS HOUSTON

PAUL HYLAND
KATHLEEN JAMIE
B.S. JOHNSON
JENNY JOSEPH
BRENDAN KENNELLY
DENISE LEVERTOV
EDNA LONGLEY
SHENA MACKAY
SEAN O'BRIEN
JOHN OLDHAM
TOM PAULIN
IRINA RATUSHINSKAYA
CAROL RUMENS
DAVID SCOTT
JAMES SIMMONS
MATT SIMPSON
KEN SMITH
EDITH SÖDERGRAN
MARIN SORESCU
LEOPOLD STAFF
MARTIN STOKES
R.S. THOMAS
TOMAS TRANSTRÖMER
MARINA TSVETAYEVA
ALAN WEARNE
NIGEL WELLS
JOHN HARTLEY WILLIAMS

*For a complete list of poetry, fiction, drama and photography books
published by Bloodaxe, please write to:*
**Bloodaxe Books Ltd, P.O. Box 1SN,
Newcastle upon Tyne NE99 1SN.**